44 Spiritual messages
Divine for Healing

by Tammy OBrien

IT'S TIME TO

Believe in Yourself

devotional

It's Time to Believe in Yourself

This divine book is designed to help you in your day and in your life. It is designed to be a daily reminder to help you heal, grow, change, evolve and move forward.

It is designed to help you believe in yourself so you can be the best version of you that you can be.

It is to help you when you are stuck, or lost, or down.

These messages I created, inspired by my divine spiritual connection are to help you, to inspire you to align with your true self and to love yourself and your path deeply.

Open the book randomly every day to see the message you may need to hear in your day.

If you are having a hard time, you need answers to something there is a message in here for you to hear at any given moment.

These messages are timeless and can be used for anytime in your life.

devotional

I hope you can be inspired by this book to help you change and to align with your life you are living.

Believe in yourself, I do, your soul does, God does.

It's time you did too.

T.OBrien

devotional

Accept What is in Front of You

You need to start accepting how things are.

Stop trying to force things to be a certain way.

People, life, and relationships change.

Accept it.

Grow from it.

Learn from it.

Move forward because of it.

Acceptance of what is takes away the resistance and lets things flow as they should.

You cannot control how things go things.

You cannot make things be how you want them to be.

Accepting means letting go of what was and what will be and seeing people, situations, and relationships for what they are, letting them flow the way they are supposed to.

Everything in your life happens for a reason.

devotional

You need to see that, accept that, and know that.

Accept what is in front of you and stop trying to make it different than what it truly is.

Ask For Guidance

Affirm this:

Today and every day on my path, I ask for guidance, help, support, and love from my angels, spirit guides, ascended masters, ancestors, and God.

I know they are with me everywhere I go, but they will not interfere on my path until I ask them to.

It's important that I ask for help every day.

My spirit guides will not infringe on my free will, but they are always showing me the way.

When I ask for help, I give them permission to step in in a beautiful way to help me in my day, in my life, and on my path.

They surround me everywhere I go.

I have an entourage of spirits and guides around me, just waiting to help me as soon as I ask them.

They take great joy in helping me.

They are happy for me when I finally start to acknowledge them and connect with them.

I am never ever alone on my path.

devotional

I know I have many angels and spirits
surrounding me.

I feel this, and I see this.

They are here with me for eternity.

They love me unconditionally.

They know me, love me, and support me, and
they are there for me every step of the way.

devotional

Believe in Yourself

Step into the power that you have inside of you.

Step out of the fear of your ego and into the light and love of God.

We all have inner power, of intuition and guidance from the higher sources of the universe.

Don't be afraid to listen to your heart and feel the love that God is pouring into you and showing you every day.

To step into this power God says you need to love yourself first, as He loves you unconditionally in every moment of your life.

You are here for the love and energy, and you are here to be guided by that love.

God wants us to become our truest self and to show that to the world.

Stop living small, and stop being afraid of your inner power.

It's there for you as a gift from God to change your life, the ones around you, and the world as you know it.

devotional

Show love to yourself and to everyone you meet.

Believe, know, and step into that love.

Believe in yourself.

Be Responsible for You

You need to remember that you come first, then others.

You cannot give what you don't have.

You have to be responsible for your own well-being, happiness, choices, life, personal growth, and self.

You need to stop worrying about what other people think.

They are not living or creating your life.

It's not your responsibility to make other people happy; that is their responsibility.

It isn't your responsibility to take blame from others; that is their responsibility.

You are the most important person in your life who can make a difference in your path and in the direction that your life takes you.

You need to remember that the love you give yourself is the most important thing.

You are responsible for your own happiness, thoughts, words, vibration, and energy.

devotional

Love yourself more every day, and don't look at anyone else's path.

Stay on your own path and own it because it's yours and yours only.

devotional

Be Satisfied in the Moment

The process of life is being satisfied in the moment.

It's the key to mastering anything and everything in your life.

Stop looking for it to be already here, and just enjoy the journey getting to where you want to go.

That's the process of life.

If you keep thinking of your lack of something, then that is what you will be manifesting into your life.

When you appreciate everything that you have and love it, you will get more of that into your life.

That's how the process of life works.

So, look inside yourself and start asking what you feel like you need right now and can't seem to stop wanting.

Probably money, a better job, a home, more love, more clarity, a relationship, or anything you are desiring.

When you change your thoughts to appreciate

devotional

and love the things you have, then you will get more of those things on your path.

This is the process of life.

The best way to live life is on purpose.

To live deliberately and in the moment.

Set your intentions every day to appreciate and love life in all ways.

Including yourself.

Change your mindset, change your life.

Celebrate Your Life

May your heart be full of love and joy today as you celebrate what you have and what you appreciate in life.

Appreciate your family, your friends, your home, your job, and the food that you eat today.

You are blessed; you are loved; you are embraced by the energy of love.

When you appreciate all you have on your path and in your life, you receive more.

Celebrate your life.

Celebrate where your life is taking you every day.

Cherish the moments you have with everyone you meet moving forward.

Today is a day for happiness, joy, love, appreciation, and abundance.

Let go of anything that isn't that feeling of love.

Let the love of life into your heart.

You are blessed.

devotional

You are loved.

You are beautiful.

Change is a Good Thing

If you feel stuck in a situation or are living in fear, these are signs for change.

The universe will make your life so uncomfortable and hard that you will be forced to move forward.

It will force you out of your comfort zone and into the new because you have been resisting the signs for so long that you need to move into a new path.

Change and growth are necessary in life to evolve and to experience new things that are waiting for you.

So, if you are in a spot right now where you are fighting change, you won't be able to resist it forever.

The universe will show you that new path and move you toward it, and you will have to face the change.

Change is a good thing; it is not something to fear but something to embrace.

It makes your life better again.

It helps you out of the old behaviours and patterns.

devotional

It helps you see clearly again.

It helps you find yourself again.

The universe is always guiding you and bringing you where you need to be.

The timing that things happen will always be perfect for you to learn and grow and move forward.

Everything happens for a reason.

There are no coincidences.

Have faith and trust that the universe always has your back.

Don't Ever Settle

There is no end to what you can do and to who you can be on our path.

It's infinite.

There is always more and more.

So don't ever settle.

Don't ever give up.

You are a powerful creator on your path.

If you focus on the vision of what you want to become, it will come.

You will step closer and closer to it.

The stronger the desire and focus, the more you will become your true self.

The more you will transform your life into a new person, a new way of living, and a new way of being.

Sometimes you don't even think it's happening until you reflect back and see how far you have come.

Don't ever give up on your dreams, goals, or life.

devotional

There is always more.

It's unlimited.

You are new every day.

Don't ever think you are not growing, changing, evolving, and transforming your life every day.

You are.

You have to envision it and feel it.

You have to believe in yourself and become it.

Drop the Heavy Baggage

Drop the heavy baggage that you are walking around with today.

It's heavy and only a burden.

Let it go, drop it, and ignore it.

It's not doing you any good or any favours.

Your past doesn't have to go where you go, and you don't need to tell people about it.

Talk about the good parts of your past if you must, but nothing more.

Stop reliving it.

People want to hear about who you are now, today, in the present.

Because that's the important person right here and now.

Go ahead and drop that heavy weight today.

You will feel so strong when you let go of it.

You will be stronger.

devotional

You will have more strength to move forward without the baggage weighing you down.

Let it go.

You don't need it anymore.

devotional

Enjoy the Little Things

The universe offers us gifts every day.

We all receive gifts of abundance, everywhere we look.

When we receive compliments, money, or material items, these are all gifts from the universe.

These are gifts meant for us, and they are a part of our abundance and desires.

We need to take them and appreciate them and thank God for the gifts we receive.

This lets the other person feel good and like they are helping us.

They are now receiving as well.

We need to receive as much as we need to give.

If we don't let ourself receive, we will make it difficult for the universe to give us what we want and what we are worthy of.

When we stop receiving, we are blocking the universe.

The big things we want in life start with the small

things, and if the universe can't give us the small things, we will never be able to manifest the bigger things we desire.

Hence, enjoy the little things, as they lead to the bigger things.

Faith Can Move Us

Today when you think something feels scary, remember God is with you.

God is guiding you and wants the best for you.

God leads you to the best things in life.

Going out of your comfort zone can be scary, but you need to step into the unknown in order to change and grow.

You have to step into our courage and be brave today.

You need to know that you have something bigger than us guiding you on your path.

You need to feel that and have faith and trust that everything is going to work out and be ok.

God gives you everything you need on your path to experience in your life.

It will come to you if you let go of your fear, which is your ego, and step into the path of trust and faith in God.

Courage is moving forward, trusting, evolving, and loving where you are going.

devotional

Fear can stop you.

Faith can move you.

Have faith, not fear.

Have love, not doubt.

God is here for you.

Surrender your fear to God and start living the life he has planned for you.

Get Into Alignment

Alignment is an important part of healing, moving forward, and keeping in a state of joy and happiness, peace, and unconditional love.

To stay in alignment, you need to feel happy, full of love and joy, and be at peace with your life in the moment.

To be in alignment with yourself and life, happiness is the key.

If you want your life to change and to be easy and to go with the flow of life, you need to be in alignment.

To get into alignment, you need to focus on raising your vibration and energy to a state of happiness, joy, bliss, and peace.

To do this, you need to be choosing yourself first.

Doing things you enjoy and focussing on love and blessings that you have in your life, not the lack of them.

Meditation, your passions and purposes, giving and receiving love, and doing the things you love get you into alignment with yourself, your life, and your path.

Alignment has no resistance.

Alignment feels good.

Alignment is the key to getting what you want in life.

Choose alignment and see your life change, grow, expand, and evolve.

More of what you are wanting will come through your path.

Are you in alignment with yourself?

devotional

Get Out of Your Comfort Zone

You have to open up your mind to new ideas and new paths.

If you keep staying the same you will never change, grow, or evolve.

Being teachable means opening your mind to new opportunities, new paths, and new perspectives.

If you keep thinking the same, you will always stay in your comfort zone, not moving forward in life.

Your comfort zone is keeping you small and afraid of moving forward.

Your comfort zone is teaching you that there is nothing more for you on your path.

There is so much for you outside of that small box you are in.

There is life.

That's where your purpose, your passions, and your life is, outside of that comfort zone you are in.

Break it open, and learn something new.

See something new.

devotional

Be someone new.

Become alive, loving your life on a deeper level.

If someone is showing up that is outside your box, go with them.

Let them show you a new way of being, living, and loving your life again.

Break open the box.

Give it a Rest

When things are not working in your life, you need to let them go for a while.

Give them a rest.

There are things in your life that are working, though.

Do those things.

Stop looking at the things that are not working in your life at the moment.

Let them go for now.

Focus on the things that are working in your life.

When you let go of the things that are not working and focus on the things that are. you release the resistance on that path.

You allow things to flow because you have stopped focussing on the things that aren't working.

You are now focussed on other things, and you allow the energy to flow freely again to the problem to bring you the solutions you need.

You let the solutions in when you focus your

attention somewhere else.

When you focus on the problem, you get more problems.

When you focus on the things that are flowing well, the energy that came from your problems will stop flowing to your path, and you can let the solutions in.

Resistance stops the flow.

It cuts it off.

Focus on the happy and good things that are going well.

Let that energy flow freely so that you can see, hear, and know the solutions that will come when you are resistant-free on your path.

Your energy goes where you focus.

Focussing on the good lets the energy flow freely into your life.

Let go of your problems.

They are getting in the way of the solutions.

Give Forgiveness

Give forgiveness to yourself, others, and the situation that you are having a hard time letting go of.

You need to take the lessons that you learn from these experiences and let the rest go.

This is why things happen to you.

You need to learn lessons in life and move forward, or you will be stuck, and you won't grow.

And that will hurt you.

To just be stagnant in life, to be living in fear, hate, anger, and frustration is hurting you so much.

You are meant to grow.

People, relationships, jobs, and experiences are here for a purpose.

They are here to help you learn from your mistakes and keep you going forward.

You are not meant to dwell on them and feel bad about yourself.

You need to forgive yourself, then let it go.

devotional

Forgive others and thank them for showing you a new path, a new view, and a new way to be.

Forgiveness allows you to feel peace, love, and happiness again.

It's the biggest step in healing your heart, mind, and soul.

Healing is From a Place of Love

When you are seeking to heal, you need to let go of the past and of the expectations of the future.

You have to forgive yourself, others, and stop being attached to the should haves and could haves.

You need to stop feeling like you are still living there.

Dwelling on the past only hurts you now.

And your past is not in the now.

Looking at the past and the bad experiences only hurts you.

No one else.

Holding grudges only hurts you.

No one else.

Being angry and living in hate only hurts you.

No one else.

Part of healing is recognizing and being aware of these things inside of you, then taking ownership of your emotions, feelings, senses, thoughts, and actions, looking at them lovingly and gently.

Don't blame others for your own behaviour, words, actions, etc.

They are yours, not others.

Acceptance and forgiveness of all parties, including yourself, is the important first step of healing.

Self-care, self-love, self-awareness, and awareness of others are keys to healing.

These can be the biggest parts of healing that you don't want to face.

You don't like to think that you may have hurt someone or that a loved one could hurt you.

But we are all humans, having experiences on this planet.

We all have egos that get in the way of being kind, loving, compassionate, positive people.

Our egos hurt us and others.

We don't need to be ashamed or hold on to guilt, anger, or hate.

devotional

So, let it all go so you can start the healing process.

Let it all go so new energy will flow to you.

Once you realize this your world will shift.

The universe will shift for you and with you.

You have to make room for a new, higher vibration and energy to come to you.

Healing energy.

Healing energy will flow when you make the intention to change.

Start your day off with appreciation, gratitude, and love.

Love heals; it is true and real.

Love cancels thoughts and feelings that are negative and hurtful.

Love is the truth of who you are, and it heals all wounds.

Healing is from a place of unconditional love for yourself.

devotional

Love yourself.

Heal yourself.

That's your power.

I Don't Have Any Worry on MY Path

You have to live in the moment and let life come to you.

Not try to make things the way you want them to be.

Life doesn't work that way.

You step onto your path in life, and then you choose.

You take another step into life on your path, and then you choose.

Don't worry about life; you can't see what's coming next, but you can choose each moment when it flows to you.

You don't have to feel lost; you just have to trust that whatever is coming, you can choose how to handle it when it arises.

If your mind is cluttered with untrue worries, doubts, and fears, you will always feel anxious and lost.

You will block the clarity with fear and doubt.

You can't live in the present moment when you

devotional

are always worried about the future that is really never here because it is always the present moment.

The now is always here, and every moment is the now.

When you worry about what's going to happen next, you don't enjoy the present moment, where you are actually living your life.

You have gotten this far and survived.

But stop surviving, and start living.

Love your life now.

Let go of worry; it is useless.

It only adds unnecessary stress to situations.

Worry just adds negative things to your life; it never makes anything better.

Stop worrying; it's keeping you from enjoying your life and from living in the now.

Living in the now is where life truly is.

There is no other time; the past is gone, and the future is always in the now.

Keep Moving Forward

Keep moving forward.

The things you left behind need to stay there.

The past is what helps you to change and grow and be on a new and better path.

That's what the past does for us.

Always.

A learning experience.

A transforming experience.

The past can't hurt you anymore.

It changed you.

It helped you.

It made you stronger.

It gave you a new perspective and a new way of being.

Start looking at the positive things the past has done for you.

devotional

There are so many positive, life-changing moments in your past.

We think your past has hurt you, but really it has changed you into a new person.

It evolved you.

It helped you.

Let go of past hurts.

They are no longer holding you; you are holding them, and they are dragging you down.

That's heavy.

Let go of them.

Be free to see the good things your past brought to you because those things are freeing you and letting you soar higher and higher.

Let Things Flow Naturally

Don't become attached to an outcome of something.

Learn to let go of things having to be a certain way.

That's conditional love.

Let things flow naturally and see where the universe takes you.

Let it unfold as it should.

If you resist and try to force outcomes to be the way you want, you will get resistance on your path.

There will be forces trying to stop you.

Stop doing that.

That's what is stopping your life.

That's what is making you feel frustrated, angry, sad, hurt, etc.

That's what is giving you nothing but grief and heartache.

Stop being attached to an outcome in your life

devotional

and path.

It is hindering your life.

You are in situations, circumstances, or meeting people in your life for a reason.

If you are resisting, you are missing the beautiful path ahead of you that you can't yet even imagine.

If you would only let go of your version of an outcome.

Attachment is what you need to let go of.

That will let your life flow easier and unfold as it should for you.

devotional

Listen to Your Soul

That negative and fear-based voice in your head is your ego.

Stop listening to that voice.

Let it go.

Stop letting it control you.

Your true inner being is the voice in your head that is full of love, guidance, support, and wants to lead you somewhere amazing.

That is your soul talking to you.

Listen to that voice.

It is a quiet and gentle, not loud and annoying and in your face.

That's your ego.

Listen to your soul.

When you're in a happy place, feeling great, uplifted, and have little to no resistance to what is going on, you will hear that little voice.

Listen to it.

devotional

Follow it.

Your soul knows what you want, and it is guiding you to it.

Your ego thinks it knows what you want, but it makes you afraid of it and wants you to stay where you are.

When you drop that egoic voice, you will hear that inner being, your soul, speaking to you.

You are letting that voice in and hearing it when you are happy and raising your vibration.

So, the importance of happiness and a quiet mind are essential in your daily life.

Meditation is the best way to quiet your mind so that you can hear the messages that are intended for helping you in your life.

Live in Love

If you are living in fear today, you cannot live in love today.

Fear is the opposite of love.

You can't be both.

Living in love is who you truly are.

Living in fear is living untrue to yourself.

You are living in your false self, your ego.

Fear isn't who you are.

Love is.

You are made of love; unconditional love to be exact.

Fear is your ego.

You are innately made of pure love, energy, light, happiness, peace, bliss, and joy.

This is who you truly are.

This is what we are all made of and who we all truly are.

devotional

Anything other than pure love is false.

It is fear.

You can't be in love if you hate.

You can't be in love if you are sad.

You can't be in love if you are worried.

You can't be in love if you spread gossip and lies.

You can't be in love if you hold grudges and dislike toward others.

You can't be in love if you are living in chaos.

There is nothing like love.

It's the energy of people, the planet, the universe, God, animals, plants, and of nature.

Fear is an illusion that you need to let go of so that you can start living your true path, true life, and true self.

Love Yourself First

Stop seeking validation and love from others.

Those people are not responsible for you.

You are responsible for you and you only.

You don't need love from others.

You need love from you.

You have love from God.

Love from the inside out.

Not from the outside in.

You are made of love.

Love is in you always to give to yourself.

Show up for yourself, and give yourself that love that is in you.

It's yours.

You are blocking it by seeking love outwardly.

It's not there.

devotional

It's not in others.

It's in you.

It's in the connection between you and God only.

Feel that love radiating and flowing to you freely from the energy of God.

It's there for you to receive.

It's yours. and it's flowing freely to you every moment of your life.

That love will change your life; it will change your path, and it will change who you are.

Love yourself first.

Love Yourself, Its Beautiful

Love yourself first always.

To start loving yourself, you must start talking to yourself positively.

No putting yourself down.

Start doing the things you love to do every day.

Your passions, your talents, and your gifts are a good place to start.

Start connecting with your higher self.

Meditate and get outside every day.

Start letting go of things that are hurting you.

Let go of anger, resentment, grudges, and hatred.

Start forgiving people because it is only hurting you, not them.

Let it all go.

Forgive yourself.

That's the most important thing in loving yourself.

devotional

Everyone has made choices that they thought were good at the time they made them.

You can't judge the past because it's who you were back then, and now it's time to change, grow, and evolve.

Forgiveness is an important part in healing yourself.

Loving who you are and not caring what anyone else thinks about you is something you have to start to do.

Be genuine, be authentic, and be true.

Once you start doing this every day, you will start to feel lighter, freer, and happier, and you will love more because you will feel love in your heart more than ever.

Love yourself.

You are beautiful.

devotional

Love Yourself Unconditionally

Loving yourself is truly how you heal.

It is the key to healing and changing your life for the better.

If you want to change, you have to do the work.

Loving yourself first is where you start.

You need to spread this message so others can heal and change as well.

You need to start knowing the truth and showing others as you heal along the way.

Do you want to know why this is so important?

Because you are loved by your creator.

Everyone is loved equally by the creator.

That energy of unconditional love flows though everyone continuously.

And when you are out of alignment with that energy that created you, you don't feel the love that is flowing to you.

You block it with other emotions that are out of

alignment with the pure, positive, loving energy that is flowing to you.

Loving yourself unconditionally is the key to pure alignment with God's energy that created you.

So, start to love yourself by letting go of anything that isn't aligned with love.

Being out of alignment only hurts you, so forgive and let go of anything that doesn't serve your purpose, that hurts you, that weighs you down, and triggers you.

Let go of it so that you can let the love you deserve into you and onto your path.

You are deserving of this love, and you are worthy of it.

Love yourself every day so that you can live your best and true life every day.

devotional

Make the Choice to Change

Every day you can choose to be the best you can, or you can choose to stay the same.

If you choose to stay the same, stuck and toxic, you will live in the pain of the past, the worry of the future, and you will stay in the same patterns that are causing you more pain.

If you choose to be the best versions of yourself today and every day, your life will change, grow, and become better.

You will love, and you will have peace and happiness.

But you have to make the choice to change.

If you stay in your comfort zone, you will stay small, and you will live in fear and worry in your egoic mind.

Your life will never move forward if you stay in your comfort zone.

You have so much more to live for than that.

If you choose to step out of that box and leave your comfort zone, you will start to bud and grow into something beautiful and magnificent.

devotional

You will take accountability for your life and your path.

You will take accountability for your behaviours and toxic patterns.

You will practice self-care, self-love, self-respect, and you will take charge of your life.

You will start to see what you need to stop doing and who and what you need to let go of that is holding you back from moving forward.

You will face the fears that your ego is instilling in you that are untrue.

You will start to have faith in your path and your life.

You will begin to love who you are and what you have in your life and on your path.

Life can be amazing if you step up and out of your fear of change.

It's not that scary; it's transforming and beautiful.

So, embrace and love yourself, feel the change of newness coming, and don't be afraid of yourself.

devotional

Life change is beautiful.

Let it flow, let it happen, and let the rest go.

It's time to live a better life today.

devotional

Meditation Changes Your Life

Meditation is one of the most powerful and important tools you can use in your life every day.

It silences the egoic mind and helps you to align with the love that is flowing to you from the universe, God, source energy.

In meditation with a quiet mind, you just are.

This is your true state of being, just to be.

There are no labels, no preferences, no judgement, and no likes or dislikes in this state of being.

That is who you truly are.

Just a soul in the moment, being aware of the moment.

In the moment of just being, you are awareness and consciousness.

That is who you truly are.

Awareness and consciousness.

A soul aware that you are in this vessel that helps you to create, learn, and experience life through the

devotional

eyes of God, here in this universe.

You are awareness.

Meditation helps you to connect to who you truly are.

This is why meditation, and a quiet mind are so important.

It also lets you hear the words, feelings, and sensations, of our spirit guides, angels, masters, Jesus, and God who want to communicate with you.

You can now align with that and hear, feel, see, know, and follow the guidance instead of the false voice of your ego.

Meditate for at least thirty minutes or longer every day.

Don't stop because you don't feel or hear anything; it takes time to get there.

It takes time to develop meditation skills and to get rid of conditions that you have built up over all your lifetimes.

It will change your life over time, and you will feel and see the difference.

devotional

Meditation is something you need to start doing every day.

Meditation changes your life.

Nobody is Built Like You

Nobody is like you.

You are designed by you.

You are a unique individual from everyone else.

You try to fit in with the crowd so that you don't stand out.

But we are all different.

We all have different talents, gifts, knowledge, and personalities, that are truly our own.

Stop hiding them.

Start being authentic and true to you.

Don't be ashamed of who you are.

You are a gift to the universe.

Show off who you are.

It's time to be different from the crowd, and follow a new, unique path that is made for you and you only.

devotional

Your personality is your own.

Show it off.

You designed it.

Start to love who you are every day.

devotional

Nothing is Impossible

Nothing is impossible.

Nothing.

If you want it, you can achieve it.

The word impossible says, "I'm possible."

If you want to heal and move forward, you have to start believing and knowing that everything is possible.

Each step you take gets you closer and closer to what you are focussing on.

Stop focussing on what you can't do and focus on what you can do.

It will be impossible for anyone who thinks negatively or thinks that something is hard.

Change takes time; it's a process.

Change doesn't happen overnight; it's gradual, so you might not notice it right away, but one day you will see it.

You are doing this, and you are changing.

devotional

Change takes willpower, dedication, focus, determination, and a positive mindset.

You are not perfect.

You will take steps backward and forward, but one day and one step at a time, you will move forward into a new path and a new person.

Everything is possible.

Nothing is impossible.

Change is beautiful.

Change is messy at first, but once you can see your wings coming out, you will fly high.

You will be beautiful and new.

You won't look back at who you once were because you will want to see what's happening going forward onto a new path.

Our Soul is the Leader

You think you have control of this path that you are on, but you don't.

Your path is controlled by your soul, your higher self, and your life.

Your soul is the leader.

Your soul is in charge.

Your soul is leading you to your destiny.

Your soul is divinely guided always.

Your body and mind are following this destiny, but you may not even be aware of this concept.

You may think you are in control.

And you are to an extent, but there is a bigger purpose, vision, and intention for your life that your soul know and is guiding you to.

That is why there is the saying, "Follow your heart."

Because that is the guidance of the divine and your soul.

devotional

Following your heart brings you to everything you are seeking and to the truth of who you are.

When you start to veer off the path of the bigger picture and destiny for yourself, your soul or the universe pulls you back by giving you resistance, negative emotions, and roadblocks.

Your soul is in charge of your journey.

You can choose to listen to your heart and follow your soul's beautiful path.

Or you can choose to follow your ego, and you will have resistance, roadblocks, detours, and negative emotions on your path.

And the hard road won't be as pretty.

You should always follow your heart, your passions, your talents, and your love because they are all connected to your divine path, life, and destiny.

Raise Your Vibe

You take our energy wherever you go.

You spread it around to whoever you meet.

Your energy is all over your path, your work, in your home, and with your family.

Your energy is transferred to others.

It flows all around you for everyone to feel.

Spread the energy of unconditional love on your path, wherever you go.

Your energy is like a signature, unique, and you attract or repel with your energy.

If it's negative, you will attract more negative energy and people on your path.

If it's positive, you will attract more positive energy and people on your path.

You will repel negative energy if you are positive.

You will repel positive energy if you are negative.

It's important to raise your vibration to a positive energy in order to change your path and life.

devotional

Stop being negative, full of hate and anger, carrying grudges, living in the past, and having toxic habits.

It does nothing but add fuel and momentum to the fire.

This is a direct reflection of your energy.

If it's negative, you need to change yourself and heal, then be a part of the change in this world.

You need to raise your vibration out of the negative flow of energy and into the positive.

Everyone plays a role in this universe, and your part is to raise our vibration to the positive and flow it to others.

Changing this world starts with you, and it will affect you so much on your path.

It will change your life today.

See Beyond Your Own View

Everyone has their own perspectives in life.

You need to be open to new perspectives.

Your perspectives are unique to you.

Your perspectives resonate with your own path.

Your perspectives are not the same as anyone else's because everyone has had their own experiences.

You need to awaken to new perspectives and experiences that can change what you perceive to be the truth.

If you are close-minded to new perspectives, then you cannot have new ways of seeing things.

Being open-minded to new experiences will help you to grow consciously, to change, and to evolve to a higher awareness on your path.

If you are close-minded and can't see beyond your own views, you become stuck in your old patterns, old routines, and you don't move forward.

Perspectives challenge your limiting beliefs so that you can discover and know the truth.

devotional

The truth of the universe, your purpose, your path, and who you truly are.

Be open to seeing something new that may help change your life for the better.

Shift Your View

It's truly a blessing to wake up and smile and say you love this day.

It's a blessing from God to see that your life is amazing and unfolding as it should.

There is no right way or right path.

There is only your path.

There is only your own unique path that you are being led down.

It's unfolding as you go.

It's unfolding as you make your choices in the day.

It's your path, it is what you make of it.

It's a blessing for you and you only.

Your path is beautiful, if you see it that way.

Your path is hard, if you see it that way.

It's all about your view of your path and life.

devotional

What are you viewing on your path?

The beauty of it or the challenge of it?

Viewing the beauty make the challenges softer and easier.

Viewing the challenges only blinds you from the beauty, and you will only see the challenges on your path.

Shift your view, your perspective, and your mindset today, and you will see your path and life change significantly.

See your path light up differently by changing your view.

devotional

Show Up for Yourself

Being true to yourself, your life, your path, and your purpose is what you are here for.

It is so important to show up for yourself, stand up for yourself, and believe in yourself.

It shows the universe that you show up for you, and the universe will in turn give you more of what you are needing on your path.

If you are putting your energy into something that isn't for you, you are wasting and draining it on something not meant for you.

Your path is your path and no one else's.

Stay true to it.

Don't let something veer you off your authentic path.

If you are genuine, your path will open up to more of that for you.

Start Filling Yourself Up

When you start to choose yourself over another that is hurting you, you start to heal.

Your love starts to turn inwards finally.

You have been so drained of energy trying to love, fix, help, support, and lead others that you have forgotten to give those things to yourself.

You are running on empty.

You're done.

Giving love to yourself is as important as breathing.

Choosing you changes your life.

The universe literally shifts the world for you when you shift your energy to yourself.

Start healing and choosing to love yourself every day.

Start filling yourself up again.

It's time for you.

Stop Looking Outside of Yourself

You are lonely because you are not putting love into yourself.

Stop looking outside of yourself.

Staying busy is also toxic.

It distracts you from your true feelings.

You need to let go and let in the truth of who you are.

Instead of keeping busy, stop and sit in meditation, feeling the peace and love that come from being in the present moment.

Go from being someone to being no one in the present moment.

Have no identity in the present moment.

Be nothing in the present moment.

Just be.

When you sit in the nothingness, you will feel the real you.

This is an important step to self-love and self-

devotional

care.

Meditation changes your life.

Meditating lets you feel who you truly are.

With daily practice it fills the void of loneliness with love, peace, and happiness as you go within and feel the love of God's energy flowing in you.

Start to meditate, love the true you, and live in love and peace.

Surrender to the Now

Stop looking at things you cannot control.

That's what anxiety is.

Stop looking ahead at life.

Live in the now, feeling the now.

There is no life outside of the now.

It's all lies.

You don't know what's going to happen in the next minute even.

Let go of that mindset.

That's what is causing you anxiety.

Control is the problem.

Surrender and trust and have faith that your life will go on as it should.

This is the key to leaving anxiety behind.

Surrender to faith.

You have gotten this far.

devotional

And you don't have control; you never do.

You can't control people or situations.

You can only let life come to you and choose in the moment what you want to do with what is showing up for you.

Letting life flow to you without doubts, fears, and worries allows you to live in freedom and in love of your life.

Living in the flow is where life is.

Living in the now, not in the future, not in the past, not in fear of it, and not in doubt of it, is powerful and life changing.

Surrender to the now and love your life.

It will change your life.

We are Divinely Led

Everything you are looking for is inside of you.

You are made with it inside of you.

The solution to everything you need is inside your soul.

It knows the answers and is guiding you, moving you through life toward them.

It is also guiding you to your purpose, lessons, soul mates, and destiny.

Your soul knows everything.

You need to take a break from your busy life and mind and let these solutions and answers in.

Meditation, connecting with nature, doing things you love, they are all bringing you into alignment with your soul.

In this place of alignment, you receive what you need to know.

Slow down to let those answers come.

Open your mind on your path to hear the guidance.

devotional

When you are busy, you can't hear your soul clearly.

When you are quiet, you can hear the inner guidance clearly.

We are all being divinely guided every day to everything we want, need, desire, and love.

Just stop and listen every day, and you will hear everything.

devotional

Will Power

Everything is a learning process that you have to practice every day.

You have to choose to make better choices and to have a different mindset.

It's a life change.

It's a new way of living and being.

Meditation, walking, focussing on the good and the positive, changing your words, and journalling your thoughts should be added to your daily routine to help you to change.

Stop saying negative things, such as: "This is hard," "It's easier said than done," and "I can't."

Quiet your mind with meditation every day.

Be aware of your negative thoughts and change them to something positive.

Stop looking at the bad and start looking at the good.

Changing your mindset is the most important thing you can do to stop your ego.

Mindset is everything.

Everyone can change and do it.

It's up to you whether you want to put in the effort, time, willpower, and dedication to changing your life.

Many people struggle with change because they don't put the effort in.

It means doing something new and different.

Change takes time; it doesn't happen overnight.

But it will be worth it for a better life and a better you.

devotional

Work on Yourself

We really must work on ourself before we can give to others.

If we are toxic people, we will be spreading toxicity everywhere we go.

To our family, our friends, our co-workers, and the world.

We need to be aware of what we are sending out to others.

We may think we are sending out love because we may be living subconsciously, when really it is going to the other person as negativity, gas lighting, or manipulation.

When we start to love ourself first, showing happiness, self-worth, respect, and unconditional love, the toxicity changes to love and beauty, positivity, happiness, joy, support, helping, good intentions, and peace.

When we are full of love for ourself, we will spread more love to our family, friends, and the world.

This is why it's so important to have self-love and self-care.

devotional

Thinking inwardly and forgiving ourself will affect everyone in our life.

Healing ourself helps to heal them as well.

devotional

You Are Free to Choose

We all have the freedom to choose our life.

We all have the freedom to see new ways.

We all have the freedom to be better people.

We all have choices.

Freedom to choose is our right.

We can freely look at the bad, or we can freely look at the good in any situation.

It's a free choice.

We are free to choose to see every situation in any way we like.

Good or bad.

Easy or hard.

Simple or difficult.

It's our choice how we see our life.

Our choices change our life and guide us to more bad things or more goodness on our path.

devotional

If we choose to look at the bad in every situation, then our life will get worse, and we will only see the bad.

The freedom of choice is ours.

Free will is a very powerful tool for us to use on our path.

Freedom to choose is ours.

Free will is in us.

So, use it to choose the good in your life, not the bad.

And use it to change your life and how you see it.

You are Never Alone

You are never alone in this universe.

You have your soul, your spirit guides, God, angels, and ascended masters all around you.

You have the beauty of the universe around you.

When you start to love yourself and who you are, your heart will fill with love for life and love for everything around you.

You will never feel alone.

You will not feel sadness in your heart.

You will feel the love of the universe, and you will feel love, worth, and happiness from within.

Your loneliness is an illusion of the ego because you are not in a space of love.

You are in a place of sadness.

Happiness comes from the love you have for yourself inside of you.

Not outside of you in people, places, or things.

devotional

Start to look for love and goodness and beauty in you.

You will be amazed by how your world and your feelings will change when you see and feel that love you have inside of you and surrounding you.

You Bring Yourself Everywhere You Go

Many people want something else to make them happy: a new house, spouse, job, car, life, etc.

That's all great if you are not trying to escape from your problems.

If you are trying to escape, the problems will just follow you to the new circumstances.

The new situations won't change your life if you don't change yourself.

All your old problems will follow you if you don't learn to change who you are on the inside first.

You bring you wherever you go.

You are the problem, unfortunately.

The solution is within, not in people, places, or things.

Change who you are, heal, then get the new life.

It always starts with you.

devotional

You Created Yourself

The power is within you to change your life.

To change yourself.

To envision yourself as the best version of you.

What is that for you?

What does it look and feel like to you?

Imagine if you could step into that dream you have of being the best you?

You can.

Focus on it.

Envision it.

Don't have a doubt that it will unfold with every step you take forward.

To do this you have to let go of the old version of you.

The version that you have created up until now is based on the vision you have had of yourself.

You created yourself with thoughts of how you speak to yourself, treat yourself, and make choices and decisions in your life and on your path.

You are your own creation.

Create a great life for yourself by envisioning what you want for yourself.

Feel it.

Be it.

You have that power.

That's how powerful you are in the universe.

You are a creator.

Start creating a better life and a better path for yourself as you move forward.

Don't look back.

Make better choices and take better care of your body and your mindset.

It's all yours to step into right now.

You are not just living life; you are creating it.

Your Path is Your Path

Your path is your path.

If you think you are struggling, you may be moving forward and not even realizing it.

Stop looking at other people's path.

Their path is not your path.

Your path is your path.

Unique to you only.

Everyone moves and flows at different awareness and conscious levels.

When you see what you need to do, you will move even faster.

The universe will provide you with circumstances that will help you see what you need more clearly.

Then you can move forward.

Sometimes it takes more time for others to see the clearer path ahead of them.

Everyone is going in the same direction, which is home to God, but each person takes their own individual path, journey, and adventures to get there.

No one else can live your life for you.

You need to experience these things in your own way, from your own point of view, and from your own perspective, in order to see the clearer path in front of you.

Thank you!

Thank you for purchasing this book.

I hope that is can help you in your day as you go.

Be inspired to change yourself and to become a better person.

Be inspired to heal, to change, to grow and to evolve into your true self.

We are all on a spiritual path, and we are all on a journey.

Let your soul lead and inspire you.

Align with the higher power.

Align with unconditional love for yourself and your path.

You have unlimited power to change your life in every moment.

Choose you and choose to change your life.

Its time to believe in yourself.

You are all beautiful and amazing souls of love and light.

Don't forget who you are.

Tammy OBrien

Spiritual Coach and Author

Please visit my website for guidance or help I am here for you.

www.itstimetobelieveinyourself.com

Manufactured by Amazon.ca
Bolton, ON

35421678R00052